D0006238

·G·R·E·A·T·
DISASTERS
THE MOST SHOCKING MOMENTS IN HISTORY

Avon Books are available at special quantity discounts for bulk
purchases for sales promotions, premiums, fund raising or educa-
tional use. Special books, or book excerpts, can also be created to
fit specific needs.

For details write or telephone the office of the Director of Special
Markets, Avon Books, Dept. FP, 105 Madison Avenue, New
York, New York 10016, 212-481-5653.

· G · R · E · A · T ·
DISASTERS
THE MOST SHOCKING MOMENTS IN HISTORY

by David Keller

Illustrations by Rick Geary

A Byron Preiss Book

AN AVON CAMELOT BOOK

GREAT DISASTERS is an original publication of Avon Books. This work has never before appeared in book form.

AVON BOOKS
a division of
The Hearst Corporation
105 Madison Avenue
New York, New York 10016

Special thanks to Ellen Krieger, our editor at Avon Books

Editor: Ruth Ashby
Associate editor: Gillian Bucky
Picture editor: Megan Miller
Consultant: William R. Alschuler
Book design by Kenneth Batelman
Cover design by Stephen Brenninkmeyer
Front cover painting by Jeffrey Mangiat
Interior illustrations by Rick Geary

First Avon Camelot Printing: November 1990

"Camelot World" is a trademark of Byron Preiss Visual Publications, Inc.

CAMELOT TRADEMARK REG. U.S. PAT. OFF. AND IN OTHER COUNTRIES, MARCA REGISTRADA, HECHO EN U.S.A.

Printed in the U.S.A.

OPM 10 9 8 7 6 5 4 3

CONTENTS

INTRODUCTION

Imagine clicking on the evening news and finding out that there is a giant asteroid half the size of the moon heading straight for Earth. Or that there is a new flu virus going around so insidious that it can kill you just hours after you've been exposed.

Imagine opening a newspaper and seeing that a firestorm is raging through Manhattan. Thousands of people are looting and stealing. Firefighters have long since stopped trying to put it out. Or maybe you turn on the radio to hear that a 150-foot wave has just washed Tokyo into the Pacific Ocean.

While none of these events is likely to happen, what makes them so frightening is that any of them *could* happen.

Almost every day there is some sort of disaster, great or small, in the news. But what is it that distinguishes great disasters from the others? It is not always the number of people killed or the amount of property destroyed that makes us remember a particular disaster. Those that we are most likely to recall are those that happen closest to where we live. Many New Yorkers still talk about the B-25 bomber that crashed into the side of the Empire State Building in 1945. Only fourteen people were killed, but the disaster is well remembered because it involved the largest building in the world and one of the largest cities in the world. At the opposite extreme, how many people outside China still talk about the 1976 Chinese earthquake in which 242,000 people lost their lives? Most people in the United States can't even remember that it ever happened.

* * *

Before our modern age, almost all disasters were natural disasters. There was little that people could do to foresee or to protect themselves from hurricanes, earthquakes, or plague. Modern technology, however, has enabled us to find out more about these phenomena. Tracking devices let us view the workings of hurricanes from satellites in outer space. We can guess where they will strike the coastline and we can make preparations or run, but we still cannot prevent a hurricane from happening. We have developed cures for many previously crippling or deadly diseases like polio and smallpox. But there is still no surefire way to prevent diseases from infecting us.

Modern technology has also given us nuclear weapons, deadly pesticides in our

drinking water, and planes capable of moving thousands of people a day—all of which can kill us just as surely as any natural calamity. Despite an abundance of food and advanced medical technology, disease and famine continue to kill millions each year.

What can we do to protect ourselves from disaster? Even with all of our technology and detection equipment, there is still not much we can do about natural disasters. Most occur without much warning. About the most we can do is take precautions against them and hope for the best. To prevent man-made disasters, there is much we can do. It is up to us to decide, for example, if having abundant energy from a nuclear power plant is worth the potential danger of a radiation leak or meltdown. Decisions such as this one are hard ones to make, but they are decisions we must consider every day.

As you look through this book, try to make some decisions of your own. What would you do if a disaster threatened you or your community?

WHEN THE EARTH OPENS UP

*EARTHQUAKES, VOLCANOES,
AND OTHER ERUPTIONS*

Most disasters happen when people least expect them. But the worst happen when people are helpless to do anything about them. Earthquakes, for example, can tear a city apart and leave hundreds dead with no warning at all. Earthquakes can occur anywhere in the world. Fortunately, scientists have determined where they are most likely to happen. Sometimes they can even predict when they might happen.

Earth scientists today believe that the face of the planet is made up of "plates" or crusts of rock about sixty miles thick. To get some idea of what these plates are like, picture what happens to a pond during a heat wave. As the water evaporates, the soil starts to dry. Finally the surface cracks open, leaving crusty dried mud that looks like a jigsaw puzzle that hasn't quite been put all the way together. But below the hard surface, there is wet mud on which the "plates" sit. You can see for yourself how this happens by trying a simple experiment at home or school. Mix clay with water until it is about as thin as pancake batter. Put it in a clear bowl in the summer sun or under a hot electric light. Within a couple of days you should be able to see the surface crack. But below the surface, everything is still mud.

The difference between the plates in the bowl and those on the Earth's crust is that those on the Earth are floating on magma instead of mud. Magma is very hot molten rock far beneath the planet's surface. The plates float on top, but drift so slowly that they move only a couple of inches a year.

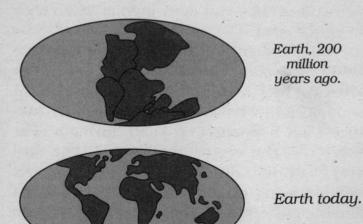

Earth, 200 million years ago.

Earth today.

That may not seem like much, but over millions and millions of years that can add up to a lot of inches. So much so that Earth looks very different from the way it did before even the dinosaurs were around. Some scientists think that the continents may have once been one huge land mass that they have named Pangaea.

As the plates float and drift on top of the magma, they are constantly bumping, slipping, and pulling against one another. It is this action that causes volcanoes and earthquakes. Two plates sometimes slip sideways as they move in opposite directions. But they don't do this in one smooth motion. They grind, push, and build up pressure until the rock slips and both plates lurch forward suddenly. On the surface, the ground shakes, buildings fall, and sometimes the Earth is pulled apart, leaving huge trenches and scars.

Perhaps the most spectacular of natural disasters is the eruption of a volcano. The scariest thing about volcanoes is that they can sit quietly for hundreds of years, not making a sound or showing even a wisp of smoke, and then, without warning, explode and tear apart an entire mountainside.

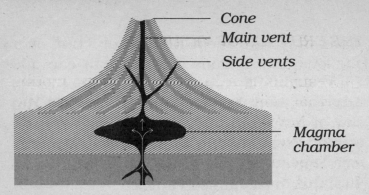

Cone
Main vent
Side vents

Magma chamber

This diagram shows the many layers of volcanic rock. At least one layer is added with every eruption.

Sometimes they bury everything and everyone near them in a blanket of hot ash or boiling lava many feet thick.

Volcanoes occur when magma breaks through to the Earth's surface. The pressure pushes the ground up into huge cone-shaped mountains. If this pressure keeps building, the whole mountain might explode, throwing hot lava and ash into the air for miles around.

In modern times, scientists have ways of predicting when a volcano might erupt, but even now, they are sometimes fooled. Almost 2,000 years ago there was no way to guess what damage a volcano like Vesuvius might do. In fact, most people didn't even know it *was* a volcano.

THE ERUPTION OF VESUVIUS

Vesuvius is a huge cone-shaped mountain that now towers 4,190 feet above the Bay of Naples in Italy. In A.D. 79, the area around it was among the most beautiful and well kept in the world. Orchards and farms dotted the mountainside. The busy trading city of Pompeii grew and prospered just to the south. On the coast to the west the resort community of Herculaneum was bathed with sunshine and sea breezes. The people who lived in and visited the area had no idea that they were on one of the great fault lines (or cracks) of the Earth's crust.

These peaceful scenes came to a sudden and tragic end one summer afternoon. The pressure that had been building up deep underground caused the mountain to crack open. It blew out ash and rock and fire with enough force to send debris twelve miles into the air. Much of the ash was light enough to stay in the air, but the heavier rocks and boulders came crashing down for miles around. The ash remaining in the air was so thick that it blocked out the sun. It looked like midnight even in the afternoon. All that day and night tremendous flames burst from Vesuvius's cone.

The next morning was even worse for Pompeii. A "ground surge" of rock, ash, and super-hot steam raced down the mountainside at over sixty miles per hour. Many citizens were returning to their homes, thinking that the eruption was over. The great wave of gas and ash killed people where they stood, choking them, burning them, and burying them almost at once. They would never learn what hit them. Pompeii lay under more than ten feet of volcanic rubble.

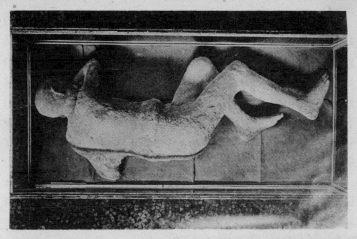

*Plaster casts of a man
and dog buried
in the ash of Vesuvius.*

There was even less shelter for the residents of Herculaneum. The superheated cloud of gas and debris that had been building up in the air over the mountain finally fell—directly on the city. Once again, an entire city was destroyed in a few moments. The huge avalanche buried or burned everything in its path.

Despite the destruction Vesuvius brought, strangely enough it left modern historians an accurate record of what life was like in those times. Once the moisture evaporated and the hot ash hardened, it left molds or casts of many of the people and household items it covered, in much the same way as fossils are formed.

Vesuvius has erupted many more times since then, but never with the same violence. In recent years, the crater has been sealed off to lessen the danger of another explosion. Even so, the possibility of the mountain blowing its top again still exists.

KRAKATOA

This mountain blew itself apart on August 27, 1883. Some have called it the loudest noise ever heard by human ears. Krakatoa's blast was so loud that several hours after the explosion, people in Australia and the Indian Ocean, almost 3,000 miles away, reported hearing the noise it made.

Despite its isolation in the Sunda Strait between Java and Sumatra, over 36,000 people lost their lives in the tremendous tidal waves that followed the explosion. Entire villages were washed out to sea, and some 6,500 ships felt the devastating impact.

The island and volcano of Krakatoa before its eruption and destruction. Today, there is a new volcano, Anak Krakatoa, arising where the old cone once stood.

MOUNT ST. HELENS

When Washington's Mount St. Helens blew its top in 1980, it came as no surprise. Scientists had been predicting that an eruption was likely for almost two years before it happened. But it wasn't until two months before the mountain blew itself apart that these warnings were taken seriously. By then earth tremors were being felt for miles around the area. Rumbling noises came from deep within the Earth. Huge cracks became visible on the mountain's surface. And finally it began to belch out hot ash and gases.

People arrived from all over the country to watch and wait. It was a beautiful scenic area, filled with lovely green forests and crystal blue lakes. Photographers, seismologists (scientists who study earthquakes), and reporters all came to watch it be destroyed.

Finally, the governor set up a "red zone" (an area into which no one was allowed to enter) five miles around the peak. Even though people protested and a few even refused to leave their homes, it turned out that five miles was not nearly enough.

The eruption of Mount St. Helens sent thick clouds of ash and smoke miles into the air.

On Sunday, May 11, beautiful Mount St. Helens exploded with a fury that few people have ever seen. Within a few seconds, the blast had spread seventeen miles north of the mountain. It knocked down trees, melted the plastic parts of cars, and killed fish in the once pure lakes with its intense heat. In all, sixty-two people were killed. Many who refused to leave the area were buried under hundreds of pounds of hot ash. Others who thought they were out of harm's way were taken by surprise. They were either crushed by falling trees or smothered by the intense blast of ash.

The ash and smoke that had been blown 12 miles into the atmosphere soon settled onto the ground. It clogged waterways and blocked roads. Whole cities and towns were blanketed with powder.

Even though the eruption killed millions of trees and animals, it is amazing to think that most of those that had once inhabited the area have since returned to stake out a new claim on life.

THE SAN FRANCISCO EARTHQUAKES: 1906 AND 1989

During this century there have been several earth tremors in San Francisco and the surrounding areas. But two devastating quakes in that city, almost ninety years apart, have been worse than any others in the lower forty-eight states.

Why does San Francisco have so many strong quakes? It's because the city lies along one of the most active fault lines in the world: the San Andreas fault. On the east side of the fault is the North American plate, which is slowly moving to the southeast. On the west side is the Pacific

*Surveying the damage wrought by the
San Francisco earthquake of 1906:
When the dust settled and the fires were
finally put out, a mass of rubble
was all that remained.*

plate. It is slowly moving in the opposite
direction, toward the northwest. But this
movement is so gradual that we can't
actually see it happening. Scientists think
that these plates are moving about two
inches a year. Two inches might not seem
like much, but it is enough to cause
tremendous earthquakes. This is especially
true when built-up pressure causes one of
the plates to slip suddenly or lurch forward.

In 1906, over 500 lives were lost in San Francisco in one of the greatest quakes of this century. Back then, buildings were not made to withstand such a shock. They fell by the hundreds, crushing many people who had been trapped inside. But it wasn't the quake itself that did the most damage. As buildings and other structures fell, they toppled many power lines and burst gas mains. Fires broke out all over the city. Over 28,000 buildings in about 500 city blocks were destroyed by the quake and fire, mostly in the downtown business areas.

If you were watching the fourth game of the 1989 World Series on television, you got to see an earthquake actually happen. One minute viewers were waiting for the opening pitch of the game and the next the cameras started shaking and the TV screen went blank. Within minutes of the October 17 quake, news cameras were back on with videotape of the devastation. Although this time the damage wasn't nearly as severe as it had been in 1906, it was still awesome to look at. The earthquake measured 7.1 on the Richter scale. Streets and sidewalks cracked. It took firefighters almost all night to put out the huge fire in the residential section near the San Francisco Bay. A sec-

*The day after the earthquake of '89:
The remains of an apartment complex in San
Francisco's Marina area.*

tion of the bridge running from San
Francisco to Oakland collapsed. Another
two-level freeway collapsed, crushing dozens
of people in cars on the lower level. At
Candlestick Park, the World Series game
was cancelled for fear that the stadium
might collapse.

Fortunately, San Franciscans are quick
to recover and rebuild their city when earthquakes strike, but there are some who
believe that sooner or later there will be one
so strong that there may be nothing left to
rebuild.

EARTHQUAKE IN ARMENIA

The worst earthquake to rock the Soviet Union in many years happened in 1988 in Armenia, near its borders with Turkey and Iran. The shock wave measured 6.9 on the Richter scale and caused death and destruction for many miles around.

Worst damaged was the small city of Spitak. One Soviet television announcer said it was as if the city had been "erased from the face of the Earth." Of the 30,000 people who lived there, only a few survived. Some estimates say that 50,000 people in all may have lost their lives. Other estimates suggest that the death toll was considerably less. Almost half a million people were left homeless.

The earthquake destroyed every building over two stories tall within thirty miles of the quake center. In Leninakan, a public school collapsed on children in the middle of classes. Fifty lifeless bodies were pulled out of the rubble by rescue workers.

One of the reasons the damage was so terrible is that the buildings in the area were not built to withstand an earthquake. Many were poorly constructed with

An Armenian woman surveys the wreckage of her demolished home.

unsupported concrete and mud. When the quake came, they fell as if they had been made of paper.

Despite the damage, the quake showed that even unfriendly nations can put aside their differences in a time of disaster. The United States raised $14.5 million for the relief effort. France, Britain, Japan, and dozens of other nations donated supplies, money, and rescue workers.

MEXICO CITY EARTHQUAKE

The Mexico City earthquake in 1985 claimed over 10,000 lives, but considering that the shock measured a terrific 8.1 on the Richter scale, it is a marvel that even more people did not perish.

Mexicans know that earthquakes are very likely to happen where they live. Mexico City is hundreds of miles from Los Angeles and San Francisco, but it is on the same fault line. Building codes in Mexico City are very strict, and engineers must demonstrate that a building will be strong enough to withstand an earthquake before it can be built.

Despite the strength of many Mexican buildings, over 500 were destroyed during the quake. Amazingly, it was medium-sized buildings, not the super-tall skyscrapers, that were most damaged. The thirty-seven-story Latin American Tower was unharmed. Scientists are still trying to figure out what made some buildings fall and not others.

Probably the hardest thing after any earthquake is locating the dead and survivors. When schools, apartment buildings, and stores collapse, many hundreds of people can be crushed under a mountain of debris.

Volunteer workers rescue an infant from the rubble of a hospital.

The day after the Mexican earthquake, hundreds of people were still trapped under heaps of rubble. Rescue workers and volunteers worked day and night to find missing people. They used any tool handy, but they had to be very careful not to crush even more people as they dug. Rescuers came from as far away as the United States and Europe with sophisticated detection equipment, like electronic listeners, heat seekers, and even trained dogs. In all they saved over 4,000 people who might have died if help had not come when it did.

THE RICHTER SCALE

In 1935, an American seismologist named Charles Richter came up with a system of rating the strength or intensity of earthquakes. His system rates earthquakes by number from one to ten. One is the weakest and ten is the strongest.

This intensity is measured on an instrument called a seismograph, which takes readings of the Earth's vibrations. Each number means that the earthquake is ten times stronger than an earthquake measuring the previous number. So, an earthquake said to measure eight on the Richter is ten times stronger than one measuring seven.

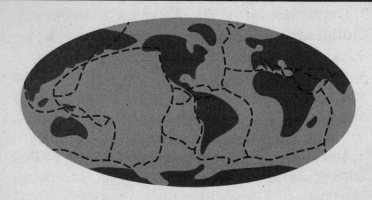

The major faults of Earth.

THE FIVE DEADLIEST EARTHQUAKES

Although the earthquakes below were the deadliest in terms of human life lost, they were not necessarily the strongest ever to shake the earth. More people are killed in earthquakes in Far Eastern countries like China and Japan simply because those areas are more densely populated than the rest of the world.

1. January 24, 1556—The worst earthquake ever hit Shaanxi Province, China. 830,000 people killed.

2. July 28, 1976—Tangshan, China. 242,000 killed.

3. December 16, 1920—Gansu Province, China. 200,000 killed.

4. September 1, 1923—Tokyo and Yokohama, Japan. More than 140,000 killed.

5. December 27, 1939—Erzingan, Northern Turkey. 100,000 killed.

WHEN THE WIND BLOWS

TORNADOES, HURRICANES, AND BLIZZARDS

Windstorms occur frequently and, because they are often sudden and violent, there's really no way for people to flee from most of them. In the case of hurricanes, they can last several days.

Hurricanes are a violent type of windstorm that usually originate in tropical regions (areas near the equator where the climate is always hot and humid). In different parts of the world they are called cyclones or typhoons, but they all work pretty much the same way. Where air pressure is very low, warm, moist air rises. When this happens, the water vapor cools very quickly and condenses into tremendous amounts of rain accompanied by heated air. The result is usually a thunderstorm.

Sometimes several of these storms combine and begin spinning in a great circle. North of the equator, they spin clockwise. Below the equator, they spin in the opposite direction. When these storms start spinning together, the air pressure in the center drops even lower and causes even more warm air to be sucked in. In turn, that makes the storm spin faster. Usually when the wind blows over seventy-three miles per hour, it's called a hurricane. Hurricane winds can sometimes gust to almost 200 miles per hour.

A blizzard is not the same thing as a hurricane but can be just as frightening. Blizzards are winter storms that occur when a cold air mass from Arctic regions meets with warm, moist air that blows up from tropical regions. When the two come together, the moisture in the warm air condenses and freezes to make snow, but the meeting also produces winds that can reach hurricane strength.

Tornadoes are the most dangerous of all windstorms. Unlike hurricanes, they do most of their damage in a very short time—sometimes in seconds. And, unlike hurricanes, there is usually little warning that one is about to strike.

Scientists know that during thunderstorms warm air is sucked up from the ground into the clouds, but sometimes other forces start this updraft spinning. Scientists are still trying to figure out why this happens. But when it does, these spinning winds begin to draw in water vapor (which is why you can see the tornado before it touches the ground). Eventually the funnel stretches out and touches down, sucking up dirt and anything else in its path. That's when the tornado turns black and awesome.

The largest tornadoes can be almost a mile wide and have winds up to 300 miles per hour.

THE BLIZZARD OF 1888

They called it the Great White Hurricane, and it was one of the most bizarre freaks of nature the east coast of the United States has ever seen.

On Saturday, March 10, 1888, people in New York and all over the country were

New York City was shrouded with snow from the Great White Hurricane.

getting ready for spring. Temperatures had been in the 50s and people were shedding their winter coats. Little did they know that Old Man Winter had one final surprise in store for them.

While everyone was enjoying the early spring, a mass of frigid air was moving down from Canada at enormous speed. From the southern United States, a warm, humid air mass was moving north. When the two collided, they produced one of the worst blizzards in modern history.

In 1888, weather predictions were not as accurate as they are now. There were no weather satellites or radar to track cloud patterns or rainfall. Many forecasts were based on telegraphed messages from other parts of the country.

On the Saturday before the storm, the weather service in New York City was predicting fair weather for Monday and Tuesday. But by Sunday night even the experts had to admit they were wrong. The wind picked up, the rain began to pour, and soon after midnight snow began to fall thickly.

By the next morning, the wind was blowing eighty-five miles per hour and the snow was coming down heavier than ever. The winter hurricane was under way.

Many people, not realizing how bad the storm really was, left their homes for work in the morning

New Yorkers struggle against the blizzard of 1888.

as usual. Some turned back. Others made it to work, only to realize that the storm had gotten so bad that they couldn't get home again. Thousands were stranded in elevated trains high above the streets.

The Blizzard of '88 continued to rage until Tuesday morning. In all, over twenty inches of snow had fallen. Everything within a hundred miles of New York was at a standstill. All transportation and communications stopped. Over 400 people were killed; many of them froze to death. Off the coast in the Atlantic Ocean and the Chesapeake Bay over 200 boats were damaged.

THE XENIA TORNADO

For Xenia (pronounced zeen-ya), Ohio, April 3, 1974, began like any other sleepy morning. But by the afternoon watchful citizens knew something was up. Dark clouds began to form to the southwest of the city. Some people may have thought a thunderstorm was on the way, but others watched in horror as one black cloud grew, then spread out and started spinning.

They had just watched the birth of a tornado that would rip through the small town. In just a few minutes it would kill 33 people, injure 1,600 others, and flatten 1,300 buildings.

The Xenia tornado ripped the exterior wall from this house – but the furniture and pictures remained in place.

With winds of up to 300 miles per hour, the twister moved slowly through the town, as if to pick and choose its victims. It crushed houses and offices, schools and churches. Huge trees were torn out of the ground and tossed aside like toothpicks.

Xenia wasn't the only town hit by tornadoes that day. Almost 150 of them touched down within hours of the one that tore Xenia apart. Towns in Georgia, Kentucky, Alabama, and Indiana were ravaged.

The tornadoes caused over half a billion dollars in property damage. In all, 315 people were killed.

HURRICANE AGNES

Agnes certainly wasn't the worst hurricane to hit the east coast of the United States. In fact, there have been several worse storms since Agnes arrived in 1972. What is unusual about Agnes is the amount of rain that poured out of the storm: about twenty-eight trillion gallons fell from the sky during the last two weeks of June.

Agnes started out as a tropical storm but soon picked up enough speed to be considered a hurricane. As it moved north, most people expected it to head out to sea where it could do little damage. But it didn't. Instead it followed the coastline, picking up huge amounts of moisture as it went. The moisture quickly condensed into rain and began to fall on land in torrents. By the time the storm turned in to shore, it was almost 250 miles in circumference.

Soon rivers were overflowing their banks. Thousands of acres of fertile farmland were quickly flooded under several feet of water. City streets were also flooded, and over 300,000 people were forced to abandon their homes.

Despite the wind and the rain, not many people were killed in the storm. But

The furious winds of Hurricane Agnes sucked this beachhouse out to sea.

one of the results of the storm lasted for a year after it was over. The swollen rivers emptied huge amounts of fresh rainwater into the Chesapeake Bay. This caused many of the oysters, crabs, and fish that live in the salt water of the bay to die. The population grew again after the water returned to normal, but until then thousands of fishermen were out of work.

HOW TO NAME A HURRICANE

For hundreds of years, hurricanes have been given names by people all over the world. But it wasn't until 1953 that hurricanes were given official names by weather services. At first they were given only women's names, but since 1979, men's names have been included as well.

There are six different lists of names for hurricanes. One list is used each year, and at the end of six years, the first list is used again. These lists have the names arranged alphabetically. Thus the first hurricane of the year is given a name beginning with the letter A. The second one begins with B, and so on through the alphabet.

There are separate lists of names for hurricanes in the Pacific Ocean. In Asia, they are usually given a number instead of a name.

NO PLACE TO HIDE

FLOODS AND TSUNAMIS

Floods have been in the news since the beginning of time. The Bible relates how Noah's ark floated through a flood that lasted nearly a year. Moses parted the Red Sea, then sent it crashing down on the Egyptians once he and his followers were through.

In modern times, Holland has learned to control the floods that plague its low-lying lands. Dikes and dams are placed strategically throughout the country to hold back the North Sea. In fact, thousands of acres have been reclaimed from the sea in Holland, giving it far more fertile land than it had just a few hundred years ago.

One of the most beautiful and famous cities in the world is Venice, Italy. It is so well known because much of the city is under water, and some believe it is slowly sinking into the Adriatic Sea. Despite the inconveniences of this unusual city, the people there have learned to adapt. Where once carriages rolled along the streets, boats now motor their way up and down the water "avenues."

In Asia and other parts of the world, fields are kept flooded on purpose to allow rice to grow. People wade through the water to harvest it by hand, as they have done for centuries.

Still, for the most part, floods are not good. A broken dam can destroy an entire town in seconds. Heavy rains can swell rivers over their banks and wash away crops.

*Rice farmers in southern France spend
hours in the water tending
their flooded fields.*

A tsunami, or tidal wave as it is sometimes called, can wash entire towns out to sea almost before anyone even knows it is coming.

How is a tsunami formed? Most start with an undersea earthquake or volcano. The shock wave disturbs the water deep below the surface, causing waves to move out in all directions. In deep water in the middle of the ocean, the wave can be miles long and move at speeds of up to 600 miles per hour. At that speed, you can easily see why people have no time to run once a wave has been spotted. When the wave nears a coastline and the water gets shallower, the

mass of water starts to slow down. But when it does, the water behind the leading edge of the wave begins to pile up higher and higher until it crashes onto the shore. (You can see this happen on a smaller scale by looking at waves on a beach.) One tsunami in Japan reached a height of 100 feet.

THE JOHNSTOWN FLOOD

Other than a tsunami, probably the worst kind of disaster involving water occurs when a dam breaks open, sending a wavelike wall of water rushing through valleys and low-lying lands. Anything in its path may be swept away.

Just such a flood happened in Johnstown, Pennsylvania, in May 1889. It caused the greatest loss of life of any dam break ever. Rain had been coming down steadily and heavily for the better part of two days. Local rivers were swelling and threatening to overflow their banks. Fourteen miles north of Johnstown, water in Lake Conemaugh, then the largest man-made lake in the country, was swelling far beyond its normal level. Overnight, the water rose two feet, and debris clogged the spillway of the dam that held back the lake. With no water spilling through, it soon became obvious that the dam was not going to be able to withstand the pressure. It was only a matter of time before it collapsed.

At about three o'clock that afternoon, it did just that. The huge dam suddenly burst and twenty million tons of water roared

*The Johnstown flood raged
through Conemaugh Valley.
Few had time to escape.*

through like thunder upon Johnstown and every town and farm in between. There was nothing anyone at the dam could do but watch. Johnstown couldn't be warned because the telegraph lines had come down in the storm the night before.

Even though the water burst out with terrific force, it took nearly an hour for it to reach Johnstown. Along the way, the torrent ripped trees out by the roots. It picked up houses, people, animals, factories, and even huge locomotives and tossed them about in one big jumble as the mass flowed toward the city.

The sheer force of the flood waters wrecked this warehouse in Johnstown, ripping up railway lines and overturning boxcars.

The people panicked, but there was little they could do but try to run for higher ground.

Many people were drowned or crushed instantly. Others were swept downstream with the wave to be rescued by those on shore or battered about until they could hang on no longer.

In all, 2,200 bodies were found after it was over. A nationwide relief effort got under way. People from all over the country sent food and clothing to those who had lost everything. The newly formed Red Cross arrived to help. Many families searched for days and weeks for loved ones. Almost 1,000 people were never found.

A TIDAL WAVE IN EAST PAKISTAN

If you've ever been to the beach and stood in the surf, you know what a terrible feeling it is to see an extra-large wave heading straight for you. So imagine what it would be like to be standing on the beach with a twenty-foot wall of water towering over your head. There would be no place you could go.

In East Pakistan, in 1970, just such a tsunami, or tidal wave, killed almost half a million people. East Pakistan (it's now called Bangladesh) had been hit with gigantic waves before, but none with the force and destruction of this one.

It all started with a cyclone roaring through the Bay of Bengal in the Indian Ocean. Winds blew at over 100 miles per hour. The storm was so fierce that it churned up a huge surge of water, aimed directly at East Pakistan.

*The Bangladesh/East Pakistan cyclone hurled
this large steamship inland to rest on a farmer's field.*

For hours the people had watched as the winds whipped and the rain fell in sheets. Then the wave struck. Twenty feet high and miles wide, it swept over the Pakistani coast and flooded over 3,000 square miles of land.

Thousands of people were crushed or pulled out to sea to drown. On the largest island off the coast, 200,000 people were killed. On many smaller islands, no one was left alive at all.

One of the reasons that there were so many deaths is that Pakistan has so many people: nearly 1,000 for every square mile of land. Most of the country is on land not much higher than the ocean itself, so there was no high ground to run to. Another reason is that the people were unprepared for the storm. There had been another storm just a few weeks before, and many people fled the coast. But the storm died out and nothing happened. This time many people thought the same thing would happen again and stayed where they were. By the time the wave hit, it was too late to run.

BURNING BRIGHT

GREAT FIRES

Everyone in America is familiar with Smokey the Bear and his message to "help prevent forest fires." The Smokey character was created because fire is one of the most preventable of disasters.

Forest fires are very easy to start. All it takes is an unextinguished campfire or a match tossed hastily aside, and thousands of acres can be destroyed. Many forest fires are started when lightning strikes a tree during a thunderstorm. Even though they are easy to prevent, they are not so easy to put out once they get going, especially if the weather has been dry or there is a strong wind blowing. To help find fires before

they spread, many of our national parks have "spotters" perched high in towers spaced so that each one has a view of a certain area of the park. If one of the spotters sees smoke, he or she calls in and a ranger goes to investigate.

Not all fires are forest fires, though. The fires most dangerous to humans happen in cities. Fires are very common in large urban areas. Some are deliberately set by arsonists. But many more are accidental. They can be started by the careless use of gas stoves, and many start in winter when people misuse heating equipment and start fires where they shouldn't. Fortunately, there are not many on the scale of the famous Chicago fire that nearly destroyed the entire city in 1871. Fire departments are much more sophisticated today, and improved communications make reporting a fire much easier. Most office buildings are equipped with sprinkler systems that can put out a fire almost as soon as it starts.

THE BURNING OF ROME

One of the greatest fires of all time was the one that all but destroyed Rome, Italy, in A.D. 64. Even back then Rome was ancient. But despite its age, Rome was a sprawling city packed with thousands of shops, tenements, and homes.

One summer morning a fire mysteriously broke out in a shop near the Circus Maximus, the great arena where chariot races were held. It spread quickly, consuming anything in its path that would burn, including the arena.

Since most buildings in the city were made of wood and burned easily, the fire proved especially hard to control. Flames

raced through the city. In the wealthy areas of the city, looters and vandals actually tried to start more fires so they could break into the abandoned shops and homes and steal whatever they wanted.

Firefighters did their best to put out the blaze where they could. In all, the fire roared for nine days before it could be put out.

NERO FIDDLES AROUND

One of the interesting things about the fire is that many people at the time thought that Nero, the emperor, had ordered that the fire be set so he could rebuild the city the way he wanted. This was never proven, and Nero denied having anything to do with setting the fire. He did whatever he could to assist those affected by it.

Nero did live up to his word to rebuild the city, perhaps making it even grander than before. But rumors about the origins of the fire persisted. One scholar wrote that Nero had not only set the fire, but had actually gone on stage and played the fiddle to celebrate the event. Even today, many use the expression "fiddling while Rome burns" to describe someone who doesn't pitch in and help during an emergency.

THE YELLOWSTONE FIRE OF '88

Except for the vast national parks in Alaska, Yellowstone is the largest in the United States. It is also the oldest, having been established in 1872. Yellowstone is over 2.2 million acres and spans portions of three states: Wyoming, Idaho, and Montana. Millions of tourists visit each year to see its many famous geysers and the thousands of wild animals that roam the park freely.

The summer of 1988, however, brought destruction to much of the park and the animals that lived there. Over 1.3 million acres were reduced to a wasteland of ashes and charred trees in the worst forest fire any of our national parks has ever had. Well over half the park was burned.

The fire started in August and spread so quickly that firefighters weren't able to keep up with it. In all, over 10,000 firefighters arrived from all over the country to help fight the blaze, but it was so bad that there was little they could do. One thing they did do was make sure people got safely away from the areas where the fire was heading. They also helped keep curious tourists from venturing into the threatened

A wall of flame jumps over a ridge and heads for the Old Faithful complex in Yellowstone.

areas, thus saving many lives. They also did their best to protect private property.

Bulldozers were brought in to clear wide swaths of forest, in hopes that with nothing left to burn, the fire would burn itself out. It didn't work. Wind allowed the fire to jump these firebreaks. Finally, three months after it had started, the fire did burn out. The first snows of the winter season helped to smother it.

There are many people who argue that the fire might actually have been good for the park. Since it is a protected landmark, lumber companies are not permitted to cut down trees there. So the trees in the park

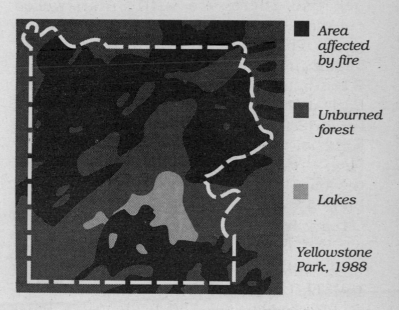

■ Area affected by fire

■ Unburned forest

▪ Lakes

Yellowstone Park, 1988

were very old. Some people think that it is necessary for a forest fire to happen occasionally so that new trees will have the opportunity to grow where the old ones had been. They may be right. There is already a new forest springing up where the old one once stood.

THE GREAT CHICAGO FIRE

The Chicago fire of 1871 is the most famous fire in American history. That's not only because of the damage it did, but because there are still unanswered questions about how it started in the first place. There is no question that the fire began in a barn owned by Mrs. Patrick O'Leary, a resident of Chicago's West Side. Early on the night of October 8, after one of the driest summers in memory, the barn somehow caught fire. Legend has it that Mrs. Patrick O'Leary was milking her cow in the barn when the cow got restless and kicked over the kerosene lantern Mrs. O'Leary had set on the floor. But after the fire was over, she swore that she and her family had been in bed asleep when the fire started. Others believed that one of Mrs. O'Leary's boarders had been in the barn and accidently set the fire.

Whatever is true about the cause of the fire, the reason it grew so large and spread so quickly is that the city had been built—and continued to grow—with little thought of fire prevention. In fact, the fire probably would not have done nearly the

LATE LAST NIGHT,
WHEN WE WERE ALL IN BED,
MRS. O'LEARY PUT
A LANTERN IN THE SHED,
AND WHEN THE COW
KICKED IT OVER,
SHE WINKED HER EYE AND SAID,
"THERE'LL BE A HOT TIME
IN THE OLD TOWN TONIGHT."

–familiar camp song

damage it did had not almost every structure in Chicago been made of wood. There were wooden stores and homes, wooden bridges and sidewalks, even wooden bricks paving some of the streets. That made the whole city a firetrap. The dry summer made things even worse.

Once the blaze got going, it burned everything in its path, forcing many to flee their homes. Looters and vandals came in behind it and stole whatever was left. The fire moved quickly across several branches of the Chicago River, which many people thought would hold back the blaze.

Firefighters tried as best they could to hold it back, but the city's waterworks soon fell to the blaze, and there was no water left. All the firefighters could do was watch their city burn and rescue as many people as they could.

*Crowds of people
flee the raging Chicago Fire.*

In all, about 300 people died that night. Many others were reported missing and never found. Over 2,000 acres had been destroyed in the heart of Chicago's business district.

THE FIVE WORST FIRES AND EXPLOSIONS

1. December 3, 1948—Shanghai, China. The passenger ship *Kiangya* struck an old mine, exploded, and sank. Over 3,000 people are believed to have been killed.

2. September 2, 1949—Chongqing, China. A fire on the city's waterfront kills 1,700 people.

3. December 6, 1917—Halifax, Canada. A Belgian steamship crashes into the French ammunition ship *Mont Blanc.* The explosion that followed kills 1,600 people.

4. April 26, 1942—Manchuria, China. Explosion at coal-mining complex kills 1,549 people.

5. August 7, 1956—Seven army ammunition trucks collide at Cali, Columbia, killing 1,100 people.

AGE-OLD PROBLEMS IN A NEW WORLD

DISEASE, FAMINE, AND DROUGHT

Plague, drought, and famine are age-old problems that can affect thousands and, in the most severe cases, millions of people at any one time. Many times they can be a result of social problems within a community. They might also occur as a result of a change in weather patterns. But like the many environmental hazards we face, there is not much we can do to escape them.

Disease can sometimes be overcome by advances in modern medicine. Smallpox, for example, was once fatal to almost everyone who got it. Polio was once a disease that crippled millions. Now there are vaccines that can prevent both diseases. Still, there are diseases that elude even the best efforts of modern science. We have yet to find a cure for AIDS, cancer, or even the common cold. Who knows, in the future there may be another epidemic on the scale of the Black Plague, one that might kill hundreds of millions before we can begin even to look for a cure.

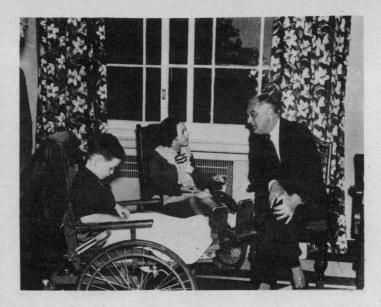

Before a vaccine was discovered, thousands were crippled by polio, including President Franklin Delano Roosevelt.

Drought and famine often go hand in hand. One growing season after another without rain quickly leads to starvation in many parts of the world, especially in poor countries. Wealthier countries like the United States have many other resources to fall back on in times of drought. They can always buy their food from other countries that have more than they need. Poorer countries are not so lucky. Those whose economy is based entirely on agriculture suffer the most when a crop fails. When that happens, they must rely on the goodwill of other countries to provide them with the food they need to live. If no one is willing to help, people may go hungry and die. And sometimes, as with the current famine in Africa, even when food is offered, it sometimes does not reach the right people.

THE BLACK DEATH

Imagine there is a disease going around that's as easy to get as a common cold. The difference is that this one can turn you into a horrible monster and kill you within three days. What would you do? Run? Hide? You can't, because the disease is everywhere.

That's exactly what happened in the year 1347 all over Europe. Most people think that the disease started in central Asia, in what is now the Soviet Union. It was carried by small squirrellike animals called marmots. These animals lived in a small area, but the fleas that they carried somehow infected the black rats that lived aboard trading ships that sailed from Asia to Europe. These same fleas gave the disease to the sailors on board the ships. When the seamen returned to ports in Europe, the disease began to spread like wildfire.

The Dance of Death was thought to ward off the bubonic plague.

What came to be known as the Black Death is also called the bubonic plague, and it is one of the most terrible diseases ever known. Usually it starts with egg-sized swellings under the arms and in the groin. These soon spread all over the body. Then black spots start to appear all over the infected person, making them horrible even to look at. It is the color of these spots that caused the disease to become commonly called the Black Death. Other forms of the disease can turn into pneumonia or infect the blood with a toxin so strong that it kills within just a few hours.

The disease spread so easily by coughing that anyone who got near someone with the plague would also get it. Even after the victim died, people were afraid to bury the body for fear of becoming infected. Eighty percent of the people who got the disease died painful deaths. Doctors who dared to treat people with the disease often contracted it and died also.

For four years the plague spread through Europe, bringing misery to nearly every city on the continent. In all, about twenty million people died, almost a third of everyone in Europe at that time.

Over the centuries, the plague has surfaced many times. Now, however, doctors have found effective ways to treat the victims.

THE POTATO FAMINE

Any number of things can cause famine or mass starvation: Severe weather, war, and natural disasters that leave hundreds of people without homes or food are just a few.

In Ireland in the late 1840s it was a disease that brought the famine that killed one and a half million of Ireland's eight million people. But it wasn't a disease that affected people directly. It was a plant disease that wiped out Ireland's potato crop virtually overnight. In 1845, this disease was accidently brought from America to Europe on one of the many merchant ships that carried goods across the Atlantic Ocean. When it reached Europe, it quickly spread across the continent. Many potato crops were destroyed.

The Irish people had depended on their potato crop for food for years. The plant grew everywhere people could find a place to plant it. In some years, potatoes had to be thrown away because there were so many. They grew other crops as well, but because the potato grew so easily and was so nutritious, it made up most of the average Irish person's diet.

When the disease finally spread to Ireland, the effects were devastating. With their main source of food gone, millions began to go hungry. Many were thrown out of their homes so that landlords could grow more profitable crops on the land the tenants had once occupied. For many, being evicted from their homes was the same as being given a death sentence.

During the potato famine, thousands of starving Irish potato farmers were unable to find work.

People died slow, lingering deaths. As many as one million people fled the country to Canada, Australia, and the United States. Before the famine had passed, over one-quarter of the country's population had either died or fled.

FAMINE IN ETHIOPIA

The famine that has plagued Ethiopia and many other parts of Africa over the past ten years is partly a result of the weather patterns that make life in that part of the

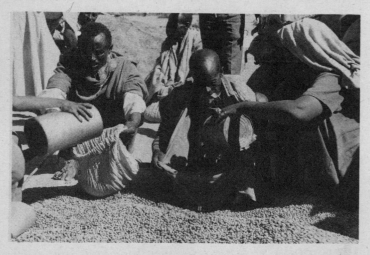

Ethiopian drought victims receive a helping hand.

world so uncertain. But the people there are starving for other reasons, too, like the nation's civil war.

Since 1982, millions of people in Africa have died painful deaths from starvation. Even worse is the fact that many of the victims have been children, who are far less able than adults to find what little food there is.

In the news, we hear more about Ethiopia's famine than any other countries', but that is simply because there are more people there. The drought and famine are spread throughout Africa. Hardest hit are those countries in the central area that borders the Sahara Desert. It is always dry there, making it very hard to grow crops. What little rain there is, is very important. But even in Mozambique, far to the south, thousands have died from hunger.

THE DUST BOWL

The Great Plains of the United States is a vast area of prairie land that stretches for thousands of square miles right in the middle of the country. Compared to other areas of the country, not much grows or lives there. Huge fields of grass go on and on as far as the eye can see. When explorers first passed through the area nearly 200 years ago they believed that no one would ever want to live there. They were wrong.

In the years that followed, people did move to the Great Plains. Farmers plowed under the soil and planted wheat and other grains. Ranchers moved in to raise cattle and sheep.

Still, it was not an easy place to live. The weather was unpredictable. At times, drought would dry up crops. Other times it would rain so much that there were severe floods. In the winter of 1932, something else occurred that threatened to move people from the area forever.

Huge dust storms started to blow. The following year they came more often and were much more intense.

The wind blew at hurricane strength, yet there was no rain. Just dust blew in these storms. Tons and tons of it were lifted by the wind and blown across the country. Crops were destroyed. The few trees there were stripped of their leaves. Entire farms were buried under dirt. One 94-million-acre area soon came to be known as the "dust bowl."

*In the 1930s, winds whipped the
arid soil of the Great Plains
into towering dust storms that rolled
through the countryside.*

In the end, almost half a million people
were forced to leave their homes and com-
munities. There was no food to be had and
nothing would grow in the dunes that the
dust storms formed.

Conservationists think that poor farming practices contributed to the dust bowl
as much as weather conditions. When farmers plowed their fields and ranchers let their
animals eat too much in one area, there

were no plant roots left to hold the soil on the ground. And since there were so few trees, there was nothing to stop the wind from blowing it all away. Some farmers have since found better and more sensible ways to use their land, but still, another dust bowl might happen again in the future.

Poor farming practices contributed to the devastating Dust Bowl.

UNSINKABLE!

GREAT SHIP DISASTERS

Shipbuilding has been an art for thousands of years, at least since people have looked for ways to carry themselves across a body of water. Perhaps the first ships may have been as simple as hollowed-out logs primitive peoples used to get from one hunting ground to another. Over the years, boats have become more and more sophisticated. Now we have speed-boats capable of skimming over the surface of the water at more than 200 miles per hour, aircraft carriers that can house over 6,000 people for months at a time, and oil tankers larger than any vehicle ever built.

Still, no matter how well built or how big the boat, there is always the possibility of a collision, a terrific storm, or something else that can cause disaster for those on board. And you can imagine the terror of being a passenger on a ship hundreds of miles out to sea and suddenly discovering that your ship is sinking. There would be nothing you could do except get into a lifeboat and hope someone came to rescue you.

Many years ago, ships were built almost entirely of wood, which meant that even a slight bump might cause severe damage to the hull, or body, of the ship. If a captain were not careful, a sudden storm might take his vessel to the bottom of the ocean before he even knew what had happened. The ocean floor is scattered with hundreds of such unfortunate ships.

Today, oceangoing vessels like luxury liners and aircraft carriers are built of steel and other metals. When you think of the hundreds of tons of steel needed to build one of these monster ships, you might wonder how they can even float. After all, steel is much heavier than water. Ships today are carefully designed by engineers who make sure that the ship is sealed and waterproof. Most are designed with their hulls in watertight sections, so that if a hole is punched into one section, the others are still secure.

Although ships are now much safer than they have ever been, no ship is completely accident proof, as you can see in the sections to follow.

THE SINKING OF THE TITANIC

It was "unsinkable!" That's what the builders of the *Titanic* claimed as it was being constructed. They had every right to think so, too. The ship took three years to build and was then considered the biggest vehicle ever made. When finished it was several city blocks long and eleven stories high. It had 50,000 horsepower engines and 159 coal-burning furnaces to power it.

Despite its size and power, however, the *Titanic* was designed to provide luxury at sea for those who could afford it. It was more like a fancy floating hotel than a ship.

The *Titanic* was also one of the most modern ships of its time. And its construction was one of the reasons its

The Titanic *was thought
to be unsinkable.*

builders thought it would be unsinkable. Inside the ship were sixteen waterproof air-filled compartments that kept the ship afloat. The designers thought that even if a few of these compartments were damaged in a collision, there would be enough left to keep the ship from sinking. But on the night of April 15, 1912, on the *Titanic*'s first voyage across the Atlantic Ocean, they would be proven wrong.

The ship set sail from Great Britain across the icy waters of the North Atlantic. All went well for two days until late at night when one of the men in the crow's nest saw that the ship was heading straight for a tremendous iceberg. By the time he saw it, it was too late to steer out of the way. The ship slammed into the iceberg and scraped past. But the damage was done. There was a huge hole in the *Titanic*'s side.

The Titanic's *lifeboat
icy North Atlan
the night before the*

It soon became obvious that too many of the ship's watertight compartments had been torn open to keep the ship afloat. Before three hours had passed, the ship was underwater and on its way two and a half miles to the bottom.

Of the 2,200 people aboard, only 700 were saved in lifeboats. Not only were there not enough lifeboats for everyone aboard, but also some of them set off from the *Titanic* before they were completely filled. Anyone who wasn't lucky enough to get on one perished in the freezing waters or was dragged to the bottom of the ocean with the ship.

ight on July hip *Andrea* ast few miles journey was sense the

passengers as another *holm*, came ht for their

s drifted in the
c for most of
urvivors were rescued.

The Andrea Doria *turned on its side before going to a watery grave.*

ship. They could do nothing but watch as the bow of the *Stockholm* plowed into the side of the *Andrea Doria*.

By the next morning, the *Andrea Doria* had sunk beneath the waves and 51 people had been crushed to death or drowned.

The *Andrea Doria* was another super ship, like the *Titanic*, which its builders thought could never sink. But as with the *Titanic*, fate once again proved them wrong. To this day, people can't figure out how such an accident could have happened.

Both the *Stockholm* and the *Andrea Doria* were modern ships equipped with radar. Both captains saw the other ship well before the crash, yet neither ship could get out of the way.

Fortunately, the accident happened in an area through which many other ships passed. When the *Andrea Doria* called for help, boats came from all around to rescue the survivors. In all, 1,600 people were saved by their fast action.

THE HERALD OF FREE ENTERPRISE

The English Channel is one of the most well–traveled bodies of water in the world. At its narrowest point, it separates the British Isles from the main continent of Europe by just 21 miles. Ships of all sizes and shapes cruise up and down the coast. Tankers, cargo ships, military ships, and ferries transport people and goods across the channel or across the ocean. The strait is so narrow that several people have actually swum across it, the first recorded in 1875.

Workers struggle to right the capsized ferry
The Herald of Free Enterprise.

On March 6, 1987, the 7,951-ton ferry, *Herald of Free Enterprise,* had just pulled out into the channel from its berth in the Belgian port of Zeebrugge. There were 500 commuters and scores of cars aboard.

Suddenly, just out of the harbor, the boat lurched to one side and sent the passengers sprawling. Within just a few seconds the boat had keeled over onto its side. Fortunately, the ferry turned over onto a shallow sandbar when it tipped. If it had not, the boat would have turned completely over, trapping all 500 people inside a sinking ship.

Instead, 184 people were killed, most of them drowned. The others managed to scramble to safety and were soon picked up by the many other ships in the area.

Like many other ferries, this one was built to handle cars as well as passengers. Once such a ferry docks, a ramp is put into position. The arriving cars drive off and new cars drive onto the ship. It is suspected that the *Herald of Free Enterprise* pulled out of its berth without first closing its bow doors against the sea. As water rushed onto the deck that held the cars, the ship became unstable and toppled over. Luckily it had not gone far out into the channel. If it had, there would have been far fewer survivors.

FLYING LOW

THE WORST AIRCRAFT DISASTERS

From its humble beginnings in the Wright brothers' bicycle shop, to the ultrafast, ultrasleek fighter planes and jet airliners of today, flying has moved up from being the sport of daredevils to being one of the safest means of transportation available.

Even so, flight is certainly not disaster proof. Every year, dozens of planes crash all over the world. That may not seem like many compared to the number of car crashes every year, but consider that there can be over 200 people in an average airliner. If one of those airliners should come crashing down from 30,000 feet in the air, there is no chance that anyone inside could survive.

What causes planes to crash? Almost every crash has a different story behind it. Engine problems are the most common reason. Sometimes flying birds can be sucked into a jet intake and cause it to shut down. Sometimes planes simply run out of fuel. In 1990, a jet airliner crashed on Long Island, New York, after it had been asked to wait before landing. Its fuel ran out and it came down in a residential area.

In 1988, on a flight to Hawaii, a huge metal section peeled away from the top of a plane and forced it to land. Sixty of the passengers were injured, and one stewardess was sucked out of the plane high above the ocean. She was never seen again.

Also in 1988, there was a tragic accident at an air show in Germany. Three pilots were trying a stunt that required them to fly very close to one another near the ground. Two of the pilots accidently clipped wings and the planes exploded. One of them crashed into the crowd of spectators, killing seventy of them.

There are many more reasons planes crash, and because of them some people are afraid of planes. But planes are a comfortable and safe way to travel. Pilots are professionals and must go through hundreds of hours of training before they are allowed to guide you through the air.

DISASTER AT TENERIFE

The worst airline disaster ever recorded was on March 27, 1977, at Santa Cruz de Tenerife in the Canary Islands. It was an unusual disaster as well, because it involved two planes, neither of which had left the ground! We still don't know exactly why it happened.

The terrible aftermath of the crash of two 747s at Tenerife on the Canary Islands.

Two Boeing 747s, the biggest commercial passenger planes made, were preparing to take off at Los Rodeos airport. One of them, a Dutch KLM flight from Amsterdam, started down the runway at high speed without getting final takeoff clearance from the control tower. In the path of the plane was a Pan Am jet. The pilot of the KLM flight must not have known it was there, because the two planes collided and instantly burst into flames. Both had just been filled with fuel.

By the time the fire was put out, all 249 people on the Dutch flight were dead and 333 on the Pan Am flight had perished. In all, 582 people were killed on both planes.

Strangely, Tenerife seems especially prone to aircraft accidents. Five years earlier, in 1972, a Spanish jet crashed there while taking off, killing 155 tourists. And in 1980, almost exactly three years after the KLM/Pan Am disaster, another plane smashed into a mountainside as it was coming in for a landing at Tenerife. One hundred and forty-six people died.

THE HINDENBURG

There are, of course, many kinds of aircraft: planes, helicopters, spaceships. But the rarest kind these days is a type of airship that has been around longer than any other. These are hot air or helium balloons and dirigibles. While balloons are meant to float through the air with the wind, a dirigible is a type of balloon that can be steered.

The *Hindenburg* was a dirigible, but it was also a special kind of dirigible called a zeppelin. Zeppelins are built with a rigid but lightweight metal frame that holds a huge envelope or bag of lighter-than-air gas. The whole thing is then covered with another lightweight "skin" that makes it look like a giant cucumber. The gas inside lifts the zeppelin off the ground. Propellers and rudders guide and steer the ship.

The *Hindenburg* was one of the largest of these ships. At 972 feet, it was longer than three football fields. It weighed 110 tons, so heavy that it took seven million cubic feet of hydrogen to lift it. It was this hydrogen that would cause the ship's destruction.

The Hindenburg *zeppelin floats slowly over Manhattan shortly before its disastrous berth in Lakehurst, New Jersey.*

On May 6, 1937, the *Hindenburg* was coming in to land at Lakehurst, New Jersey, after a long voyage from Germany. There were ninety-seven people on board. It was just pulling close to the mooring tower when the whole ship exploded. Actually, it was the hydrogen that exploded. Although hydrogen is lighter than air and works well to make things float, it burns very easily. The fire caused the whole ship to collapse and fall 300 feet to the ground, burning all the while. Thirty-three people were killed and many more were injured, including those trying to rescue the survivors inside the burning zeppelin.

Some people still think there might have been a bomb planted on the ship, but an investigation later showed that the most likely cause of the explosion was an electrical storm.

BOMBER HITS EMPIRE STATE BUILDING

One of the most spectacular, if not the most deadly, moments in New York history has to be the Saturday morning in July 1945 when a World War II B-25 bomber slammed into the side of the Empire State Building. At that time it was the tallest building in the world.

Miraculously, only fourteen people were killed in the accident. If it had not happened on a weekend, there would have been 15,000 office workers in the building, and many more surely would have died.

It started with a routine flight from Massachusetts to New Jersey. Pilot William Smith and two passengers were flying over New York when the air traffic controllers at

New York's La Guardia airport advised them to land there because of bad weather conditions. There was a thick, low-lying cloud cover that kept visibility to a minimum. Since the New Jersey airport was just a few miles farther on, the pilot ignored the advice and kept going.

What happened next is still a mystery. In the clouds, the pilot probably lost his sense of direction. Flying over Manhattan, he lowered his landing gear, thinking that he was approaching the airport. In reality, he was flying in between the skyscrapers. By the time the pilot realized where he was and started desperately to climb away from the danger, it was too late. The Empire State Buil-

The gash ripped in the Empire State Building by the B-25 bomber that plunged into its north face.

ding was right in front of him and there was no way to get around it.

The bomber hit the building seventy-nine floors above the ground. It exploded almost instantly, killing everyone in the plane and eleven people working in the building. The impact sent the plane's engines crashing through walls and offices, spilling burning fuel everywhere. Part of one of the engines and the landing gear were flung all the way through the building and out the other side. It crashed through the roof of another building far below.

Despite the damage, firemen were able put out the fires in under an hour and 1,500 people were evacuated from the building safely. The hole left in the building tooks weeks to repair, but if you look at the spot today, you would never know how close the majestic building came to being burned to the ground.

THE VINCENNES *AND AIR IRAN*

The accident that caused the deaths of 290 people on an Air Iran commercial flight in July 1988 was caused by one of the most ghastly mistakes of our century.

The Iranian plane had taken off on a regularly scheduled flight. Miles away, floating in the Persian Gulf, the United States' military ship *Vincennes* was tracking its every move on sophisticated radar equipment. On the radar screen, the plane looked like a small dot approaching the ship.

That's when things began to go wrong. The U.S. Navy ship identified the plane as being an Iranian Air Force F-14 Tomcat fighter, a heavily armed war plane that could easily sink the *Vincennes* if it got close enough and attacked. The *Vincennes* tried to keep that from happening by launching two missiles at the plane. Moments later and seven miles away, the plane was blown out of the sky. The problem was that it wasn't a jet fighter. In fact, the commercial flight posed no threat at all to the Navy ship.

Most people realized that the captain of the *Vincennes* had only been trying to protect his ship, but that couldn't bring back the 290 innocent people lost in the accident. Even today, Iran blames the United States. After all, it was Iranian citizens who were killed.

Just five years before, in 1983, there had been a similar accident. A Korean airliner accidently crossed into Soviet airspace. Jet fighters were quickly sent up to shoot it down over the Pacific Ocean. Once again, the tragedy was a result of a plane being misidentified as hostile. The United States still blames the Soviet Union for this tragedy.

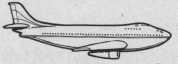

Air Iran Passenger Jet

F-14 Tomcat Fighter

THE FLIGHT OF DAEDALUS AND ICARUS

One of the earliest recorded air disasters occurs in Greek mythology. Icarus was the son of Daedalus, a sculptor and architect who had fallen out of grace with King Minos of the island of Crete. When Minos imprisoned the two on the island, Daedalus devised a means of escape unheard of at that time: they would fly off the island like birds. Daedalus formed two pair of wings from feathers and wax and strapped them onto Icarus and himself.

Before they took off, Daedalus warned Icarus not to fly too close to the sun or his wings would melt. Back then, people believed the higher you went in the sky, the hotter the sun got.

Icarus's new freedom in flight proved to be too much for him to handle. Overjoyed with his new ability to fly, he went higher and higher until the wax holding his wings together melted and he tumbled into the sea to his death. Daedalus managed to finish the flight and escape.

THE FIVE WORST AIRCRAFT ACCIDENTS

It is interesting to note that nine of the ten worst air accidents have occurred within the last fifteen years. Air travel has become much more common in that time. Passenger airliners are larger and hold an ever increasing number of people. Traffic in the air has become heavier, and more sophisticated technology means that a greater number of things can go wrong.

1. March 27, 1976—Santa Cruz de Tenerife, Canary Islands. Two passenger jets collide on runway and 582 people are killed.

2. August 12, 1985—Japan Air Lines Boeing 747 crashes into a mountainside and 520 people are killed.

3. March 3, 1974—Paris. DC-10 crashes into a forest just after takeoff and 346 people are killed.

4. June 23, 1983—Air India Boeing 747 explodes over the Atlantic Ocean, killing 329 people.

5. August 19, 1980—Riyadh, Saudi Arabia. When a burning jet liner is forced to land, 301 passengers unable to get out of the plane are killed.

THE FINAL FRONTIER

SPACECRAFT ACCIDENTS

So far, only the Soviet Union and the United States have built spaceships capable of launching men into space, but other countries are planning their own space programs to begin in the very near future. Perhaps with an increasing number of people going up into space there will be more accidents. But so far, there have been only a small number of them.

When the U.S. and Soviet Union first began launching men into orbit, only one or two went at one time. Now, with the space shuttle, the crews are much larger. The space shuttle *Challenger* had seven aboard when it exploded. It had been fifteen years since another astronaut had died in space.

THE APOLLO TRAGEDY

On January 27, 1967, the United States's space program had its first casualties. It happened on the first manned mission of the Apollo project, the same project that would later send men to explore the Moon.

The charred exterior of Apollo 12 command capsule.

Strangely enough, the disaster struck before the spacecraft even left the ground. Three astronauts (Roger Chaffee, Virgil Grissom, and Edward White, who had been the first person to "walk" in space) were in the nose cone of the Apollo and preparing for lift-off.

Meanwhile, down on the launchpad, an electrical fire had broken out. It quickly spread and burned the capsule in which the astronauts were strapped. The fire spread so quickly because the capsule was filled with pure oxygen and the interior was flammable plastic. There was no time for them to escape, and no one was close enough to reach them in time.

It was a disaster that reduced much of the optimism members of the program had had. It showed that despite the many achievements people had made in space, there was always room for something to go wrong. Fortunately, the Apollo program continued and a little over two years later, Neil Armstrong was walking on the Moon, the first person ever to do so.

THE CHALLENGER DISASTER

The explosion of the *Challenger* space shuttle is one of the most memorable events of our time. It was made even more memorable because it was one of the few disasters to actually be televised live.

It seems everyone watches whenever a space shuttle is launched. NASA launched the first shuttle in April 1981. The shuttle was the first spaceship ever built that could be reused. The shuttle takes off by riding piggyback on rocket engines that boost it into space. Once there, the crew launches satellites and performs scientific experiments. When the astronauts are ready to return to Earth, they reenter the atmosphere and fly back down just as if the shuttle were a regular airplane. Shuttles can be used up to 100 times and can stay in space up to 30 days.

Horrified spectators watch as the Challenger
explodes just seconds after launch.

But on its tenth mission, tragedy struck the shuttle. It was a clear but cold January morning in 1986 when the seven astronauts climbed into the *Challenger* space shuttle. Everyone was excited because this was the first time an ordinary citizen was to go into space. Her name was Christa McAuliffe, and she was a schoolteacher from New Hampshire.

Millions watched as the countdown began. The shuttle took off right on schedule. But just over a minute into the flight, high above the Atlantic Ocean, the spaceship burst into flames and exploded. All seven astronauts were killed instantly. It would be over two years before another shuttle was launched. In the meantime, it was discovered that a defect in one of the rocket boosters had caused the explosion.

LAIKA: THE FIRST DOG IN SPACE

In 1957, back before anyone had ever left the Earth's atmosphere, scientists were concerned about what effects being launched into space would have on humans. Some thought that the acceleration of a spaceship to the 17,000 miles per hour needed to escape the Earth's atmosphere might be too much for the human body to handle. Others thought that astronauts might get sick because of the lack of gravity in outer space.

To test all of these things, scientists in the Soviet Union chose to send up a dog first. The one they chose was named Laika, and she was launched in the Sputnik 2 on November 3. Laika was strapped into the spaceship and hooked up to monitors so that the scientists on earth could observe her reactions. Fortunately, Laika suffered no ill effects, so the scientists determined that it must be safe to send up humans. Thanks to Laika paving the way, hundreds of men and women have been safely launched into space. The sad part of the story is that the space capsule in which Laika was launched was not designed to return to earth. Laika died when her air ran out.

GALLONS OF GOO

GIANT OIL SPILLS

Even a small oil spill can cause a lot of damage to marine life and animals that live on shore where a spill washes up. But when a large one happens, the effects can be felt for years, perhaps even for a lifetime.

Many oil supertankers are the length of several football fields.

Crude oil is found deep underground in places all over the globe. Alaska, Mexico, and Nigeria, for example, have plentiful supplies. But most of it is found in Middle Eastern countries like Saudi Arabia, Oman, and Iran. Many countries have no source of oil. So if they want to use it, they have to buy it from other nations and transport it to their own country.

Oil is carried for hundreds or even thousands of miles in huge ships called supertankers. If you set the largest of these supertankers on its end, it would be taller than the Empire State Building. As large as these ships are, they do sometimes break open. If a tanker runs into shallow water and the hull rips open, or if one hits another ship, oil spills out into the open sea. Since oil is lighter than water, it floats on the surface and spreads out in whatever direction the current carries it. Since most wrecks happen close to shore, it doesn't take long before the oil washes up onto beaches.

Oil spills are terribly hard to clean up. In the open sea, oil can sometimes be contained in one area by keeping it trapped inside a barrier that floats on the surface of the water. But once the oil reaches shore, it coats everything it touches with a goo that's almost impossible to clean. Fish die when it gets in their gills. Ducks and seabirds can't fly after getting it on their wings.

It is possible to prevent oil spills, but it is very costly to clean them up. And once the damage to the environment is done, it cannot be reversed at any price.

PORTSALL, FRANCE

The history of oil pollution disasters does not go back very far. In fact, no one thought much about them until just a few years ago. It might have been the disastrous spill off the coast of Portsall, France, that made people realize exactly what kind of damage can be done to our delicate environment in a matter of moments.

The supertanker *Amoco Cadiz* was carrying 230,000 metric tons of crude oil that had been loaded into it in the Persian Gulf. It was on its way to Rotterdam, the Netherlands, where it would unload its cargo of oil. But off the coast of France, the weather changed, and the sea began to churn. The ship's steering system failed and

After the supertanker Amoco Cadiz broke in two, thousands of birds and fish were killed and the coastline was turned into a black mud.

soon the ship ran aground off the rocky coast. The rocks tore a hole in the belly of the ship, and all of the oil inside poured out into the ocean. Finally, the ship actually broke in half.

The oil was churned about in the sea until it had spread out enough to cover 100 miles of the French coastline. Millions of marine animals and birds were killed. Oil-covered fish and shellfish washed ashore by the hundreds of thousands. Mile after mile of beach was ruined. Professional fishermen in the area were all but put out of business.

THE EXXON VALDEZ *DISASTER*

The United States is the largest energy consumer on Earth. It uses up almost one-quarter of all the energy produced in the world. Much of it is produced within this

Workers clean rocks one by one along the Alaskan shoreline.

country: coal from mountainous states like Kentucky and West Virginia; oil from deep beneath the ground in places like Alaska and Texas. Still, hundreds of millions of gallons of oil are shipped from other countries every year.

That makes oil spills as likely to affect the United States's shorelines as anywhere else. While there have been many, the worst one ever happened in March 1989. The 937-foot-long supertanker *Exxon Valdez* accidently ran aground in Prince William Sound off the coast of Alaska. All ten million gallons of the crude oil it was carrying spilled out into the ocean and formed a huge oil slick on the surface. It soon washed onto the Alaskan shoreline and coated it with muck.

Even though there was a tremendous cleanup effort, it was not enough. Millions of animals died, including thousands of seals and endangered species like the sea otter. And 100 miles of scenic Alaskan coastline were spoiled, possibly for as long as we live. People are still trying to clean up the mess, but as with any oil spill, once the damage has been done, it is almost impossible to reverse.

GLOWING, GLOWING, GONE

DISASTERS IN A NUCLEAR AGE

There are disasters that can't be seen or heard, but are disasters nonetheless. Chemical factories, pollution, and nuclear power plants all hold the potential for widespread and unknown disaster. Yet we've spent many years with these in our midst.

Nuclear power plants are now nearly everywhere in the country. They provide us with electricity without having to burn coal or oil like other kinds of power plants. Therefore they don't pollute the atmosphere on a daily basis. But the threat of radioactive contamination is something we must all live with. Even though some people would like to assure us that nuclear plants are absolutely safe, we know from history that things can go wrong. Radiation can leak and contaminate the environment for hundreds of miles around. And what do you suppose would happen if a nuclear power plant were ever in the middle of an earthquake or other natural disaster?

There are other unseen disasters waiting to happen. Chemical plants produce pesticides and ingredients that are used in products we see every day. Paints, plastics, household cleaners, and many other items are products of the chemical industry. Unfortunately, when people finish using these products, they are thrown into landfills or toxic-waste dumps. There they may break back down into chemicals and seep into the ground, where they can get into our water supply. Pesticides can spread in a similar way. They might seep into the ground after farmers spray them on their crops, or they might not get washed off the crops that find their way to the market.

There are many ways that pesticides can find their way onto your dinner plate.

Asbestos is a soft mineral that was once used for making things fireproof. But scientists discovered that it could cause lung cancer if it is inhaled. It is so deadly that a particle the size of a piece of dust can cause cancer decades after it enters your lungs. Asbestos is now banned in all building construction material, but it still poses a problem when it has to be removed from older homes. In many cases, asbestos that was installed in buildings many years ago is simply enclosed in an airtight casing to prevent the dust from affecting workers.

There are many other invisible pollu-
tants in the air, in our water, and even in
the soil that supports our food system. Who
knows exactly how much we are actually
putting into our bodies without even realizing what we are doing?

CHERNOBYL

It is the most famous and by far the
worst nuclear accident ever to happen. It is
also our best example of how powerless we
are against the hazards of radioactivity.

The Chernobyl nuclear power station
near Kiev had four nuclear reactors and
was one of the largest and most productive
in the Soviet Union. It generated electricity
for millions of people in the Ukraine, a
heavily populated republic in the western
part of the Soviet Union.

On April 26, 1986, there was an explosion and fire in one of the reactors. The fire
nearly caused a meltdown, which happens
when the fuel rods in the reactor core begin
to melt. If this happens, it is possible that
they can heat up so much that they melt

A Soviet girl demonstrates a tree-leaf that was deformed as a result of radiation from Chernobyl.

through the plant down into the earth. Extremely high levels of radiation could be released. The meltdown was prevented by pouring sand and then concrete into the reactor to seal it, but not before much radiation was released into the atmosphere.

Although the accident happened in the Soviet Union, it was Sweden that first discovered that there had been a radioactive leak. Officials there detected high levels of radiation that had spread out in a huge invisible cloud from Chernobyl. Within a week, the cloud had blanketed much of Europe and the western Soviet Union. Countries all over the world criticized the Soviets for trying to keep the accident quiet and for being so slow to clean up. By the time the accident was discovered, the cloud was breaking up and spreading all over the world.

After the accident became known, many countries began testing animals like sheep and cows for radioactivity. In animals that fed on grass and other plants, radioactive levels were found to be much higher than normal. This meant that their meat was unsafe for humans to eat and their milk unsafe for people (especially babies) to drink. Farmland and crops were ruined.

Even though people were not killed immediately in this almost invisible disaster, 300 have died since. It is impossible to guess how many more might die early deaths from cancer as a result. Estimates go as high as 30,000 in Russia. There is also a possibility that there will be an increase in the number of birth defects in the area in the years to come.

THE BHOPAL INCIDENT

Pesticides are among the most dangerous chemicals on earth. They are designed for no other purpose than to kill unwanted insects and small animals like rats and mice. But they are also quite dangerous to humans. You can find pesticides in many common places: in household bug spray, on farms, even in city parks. They are also found in many places where they shouldn't be—places where they can be harmful to humans.

When farmers spray their crops with pesticides, much of it washes off when it rains. Some of it seeps down deep into the soil and gets into our water system. Whatever stays on the surface runs off into

*These Bhopal women's eyes were seared by the
Union Carbide chemical leak.*

rivers and streams, polluting them and poisoning the fish. Sometimes the pesticides don't come off the crops even after they are harvested and washed. You've probably even eaten or drunk pesticides and don't even know it!

In the city of Bhopal, India, there was a disaster involving pesticides in 1984 that shows just how deadly these chemicals can be. An accident at a pesticide factory owned by the Union Carbide company allowed a poisonous gas to leak out of a storage tank. It quickly spread for miles, and settled down over the city surrounding the factory. Two thousand people died, many of them in their sleep. But many more suffered. People were running through the streets, foaming at the mouth or writhing on the ground. Over 180,000 people had to be treated in hospitals.

The factory was closed, and several Union Carbide officials were held responsible for the accident. Amazingly, just a few days after the plant was closed, it was announced that it would reopen, causing nearly 200,000 people to flee in fear for their lives.

WEIRD DISASTERS

What makes a disaster weird? Several of those listed here might easily fit into other categories, but in every case, there is something about them that makes them unusual. There are many one-of-a-kind occurrences. There are also disasters so bizarre that no one has been able to figure out why or how they happened. Finally, there are a few disasters that, like the killer bees, we bring upon ourselves.

Perhaps the best kind of weird disaster is the kind that comes from your imagination—the kind in which no one really gets hurt. Science fiction books and movies are full of this kind of disaster: runaway rollercoasters, giant meteors on a collision course with Earth, city-stomping monsters like King Kong and Godzilla. Maybe you can even come up with a few of your own.

THE MYSTERY IN LAKE NYOS

Some of the most bizarre freaks of nature happen in places you might never expect. In 1986 almost 2,000 people and hundreds of thousands of animals were killed in an accident that may never be fully solved.

Lake Nyos was a beautiful blue mile-wide crater lake in Central Africa before the disaster. It was surrounded by a few small villages and farms. People had lived in the area for perhaps thousands of years, but for many of those years there had been a huge gas bubble building up in the bottom of the lake.

The mysterious gas bubble erupting from Lake Nyos instantly killed about 1,200 people and hundreds of thousands of animals.

No one knows what caused it to burst to the surface, but it is certain that no one could have predicted it. About 9:00 P.M. on August 21 the residents heard a rumbling that must have sounded like thunder. No one was surprised since it was the rainy season and thunderstorms were frequent. But it wasn't thunder. The gas bubble had broken loose, and within a few moments every living thing that breathed it in died. It affected nearly every animal, even birds and insects. Since the gas was heavier than air, it didn't rise and disperse in the atmosphere like some gases might, but it sank to the ground where it would do the most damage. In the tiny village of Nyos, only four people were left alive.

Amazingly enough, the area is in such a remote part of the world that it was nearly two days before anyone from the outside even knew what had happened. Since there were almost no human survivors, there was no one left to report the story. It had to wait until someone wandered into the area from the outside.

What caused the bubble is still a mystery. The local people thought it might have been angry spirits, but most scientists think the bubble was freed by a mild earthquake or volcanic activity. The real cause may never be known.

KILLER BEES

Killer bees are a disaster in a different sense of the word. They don't swarm down and wipe out entire cities. They don't carry dangerous diseases like the fleas that brought the bubonic plague to Europe. But they are frightening to think about. So much so that entire books have been written about them. In fact, there's even a horror movie or two about them.

Killer bees are a genetic disaster. Until a few years ago, there was no such thing as a killer bee. They came about when forty-six African queen bees were brought to Brazil as an experiment to see if they could help the local bee population produce greater amounts of honey. Unfortunately, some of these bees got loose and began to breed in the wild with the native bees. This was something they couldn't do before because the two groups were an ocean apart.

A "normal" bee will not sting unless it or its queen bee is threatened. But killer bees will attack at the slightest disturbance. People are afraid of them for two reasons: They sting more often than their European-bred relatives, and they attack in swarms or groups, in much the same way that hornets go after anyone who disturbs their nests.

Although killer bees started in Brazil, they have been spreading throughout South and Central America through the years. Since the African bees were introduced in 1956, several hundred people have been killed by them. Now they are just a few hundred miles south of Texas, and unless the change to a cooler climate has an effect on them, they will spread throughout the United States in the next few years.

EXPLOSION IN SIBERIA

Certainly the most remarkable mystery of this century was a disaster that probably didn't kill anyone, and one that cannot be explained to this day.

On June 30, 1908, in a remote section of Siberia in the Soviet Union there was a devastating explosion equal to the blast of about thirty tons of TNT. The blast knocked down trees for an area of about twenty-five square miles.

Trees were blasted and sheared off but left standing at the center of the Siberian explosion.

People who saw the disaster from a distance said a huge flame had shot up from the horizon. This was followed by the sounds of a terrific explosion. The ground shook as if there were an earthquake. In the days and weeks that followed, dust blown high into the air from the explosion reflected the sun's light even in the middle of the night, making it seem like daytime twenty-four hours a day.

No one knows for sure what caused the explosion, but almost everyone agrees that it did not originate from something on Earth. Some suppose that it might have been caused by a meteor or comet. But an investigation of the crash site showed no crater that would have been caused by the impact of a meteor. There were just fallen and burned trees, but it seems as if nothing actually struck the Earth. Even more mysteriously, in the area just below where the impact would have occurred, trees were actually left standing. This has led some speculators to believe that whatever it was exploded just before it hit the Earth.

Some people have even guessed that it might have been an alien spacecraft that fell to Earth. But eighty years have passed since the explosion, and with little evidence to back up any theory, we'll probably never learn what really happened.

THE DEATH OF THE DINOSAURS

We may never learn the true reason why all of the dinosaurs suddenly died out over sixty-five million years ago. But there are several interesting theories, some more believable than others.

Dinosaurs lived during the Mesozoic Era and roamed the Earth for over 160 million years. They came in all shapes and sizes, from the size of a small bird to the eighty-foot-long giants. They were very adaptable creatures. We know this because their bones are found on every continent in the world, except Antarctica. We also know that some ate only vegetation, while others devoured flesh.

But what caused them to disappear? The earliest discoverers of dinosaur bones could not even explain what they were or where they came from, much less why they had vanished. But soon there was one theory after another.

One of the earliest guesses supposed that the dinosaurs were stupid creatures with very small brains. Thus, they were eventually outwitted by smarter, though smaller creatures. Now, however, we know that the dinosaurs were no less intelligent than other animals of their time.

Another favorite theory is that the many volcanoes that were scattered all over the planet became so active that the gases and ash that came spewing out of them changed the Earth's atmosphere. Earth's protective layer of ozone (an invisible gas that protects against harmful radiation from the sun) might have been weakened long enough to kill the dinosaurs.

Still another theory suggests that the Earth's climate might have suddenly changed, making it much cooler than before. The dinosaurs, not having hair like mammals, might not have been able to adapt to the cold weather.

In recent years the favored theory is that a giant asteroid or comet struck the Earth millions of years ago. If such an object crashed through our atmosphere, the dust thrown up from the impact might have blocked out the sun for many months.

Without the sun's warming rays, all but the hardiest animals may have perished. This theory gained support whcn, in 1987, scientists discovered an underwater crater off the coast of Nova Scotia measuring twenty-eight miles across.

Through the years, many other theories have been proposed and rejected by some, accepted by others. But we'll probably never know the whole truth. Who knows? If it was a sudden catastrophe that killed the dinosaurs, it's possible that they might still be around today if it hadn't happened.

KILLER FOG IN LONDON

More than any other place in the world, London is known for its fog. It has been something that Londoners have lived with and tolerated for centuries. Some think it is charming and quaint, but mixed with smoke it is something else all together. The two combined become smog (SMoke + fOG), a dangerous gas that affects anyone who breathes it.

Other cities have similar air pollution problems: Los Angeles, Mexico City, and

A helpful London policeman directs a visitor wearing a protective mask through the thick smog that blanketed the city

Athens, Greece, are a few of the world's smoggiest cities. What happened in London in December 1952 shows just how devastating smog can be and provides a valuable lesson for other cities.

It began when a mass of warm Atlantic air settled in over London. Cool, moist air was trapped beneath. A thick, dense fog soon formed, but unlike other times, there was no breeze to blow it away after a few hours. In fact, the fog hung in the air for several days. And all the time it held down airborne particles of soot and smoke that came from stove and car exhausts.

Soon, the smog became so thick that people couldn't see their own feet as they walked. Buses and trains inched along through the murk. There were many accidents and collisions. Some drivers simply left their cars when the going got too rough. People began piling into hospitals, complaining of breathing problems. Some estimates show that some 4,000 more people than usual died that December. Thousands of others suffered from the long-term effects of the haze.

Finally, four days after the smog settled, it began to clear, but it had left many shaken lives in its wake. Even so, some good did come of the disaster. In 1956 a clean air act was passed in Britain. This new law required businesses to lessen the amount of pollution they released into the air. It even required the government to help people switch from burning coal for heat and power to using less polluting fuels. London is cleaner now, and there are fewer heavy fogs. But it will be many years before people change their ways and end air pollution forever.

AFTERWORD

Now you've taken a look at some of the worst disasters of this or any other time. But what kinds of disasters might the future bring?

In the United States, any number of things could bring about a calamity that might change the way we live forever. Some people fear that a tremendous earthquake might strike the West Coast, causing a huge rift along the San Andreas fault. Some have even speculated that the major cities of California (San Francisco, Los Angeles, and San Diego) might tumble into the ocean.

On the East Coast, some fear that one day there may be a hurricane with winds more powerful than anything we have ever seen before. The tide might rise enough to allow salt water to flood coastal cities and destroy inland farmland. It might even be powerful enough to reform the entire coastline, covering many areas with water that had previously been dry land, and leaving the sea bottom high and dry in others.

But aside from some natural calamity that might wreak devastation on us in an instant, there are far more insidious ways that we might be done in on a huge scale.

Overpopulation, pollution, and our own destruction of our and other species' habitats are disasters in the making. But we don't often think of these problems as disasters unless they produce some catastrophe.

There are 5 billion people alive on Earth right now, and within your lifetime that number is likely to double. The fact that there are so many of us tells us that we have to be very careful how we lead our lives, not only for our own benefit and safety, but for that of future generations.

There are disasters that we are completely unable to prevent. But we can prevent our air from being polluted, our topsoil from washing into the sea, and valuable plants and animals from becoming extinct.

We also have a voice in whether to allow governments to deny plentiful food to the starving, whether to allow ourselves to be dependent on dangerous technology, and whether to continue to threaten each other with nuclear warfare.

The choice is ours.

GLOSSARY

AIDS Acquired Immunodeficiency Syndrome. A viral infection which causes the human immune system to fail.

ARSON The deliberate setting of fires.

ASBESTOS A soft mineral that separates into fibers. Used for many fireproofing purposes.

ATMOSPHERE The gases that surround a planet, such as the Earth.

BERTH The space where a ship lies when at anchor.

COMET A celestial body, with a starlike head and a tail of light, which orbits about the sun.

CONE The top of a volcano.

CYCLONE A violent, destructive rotating wind.

DIRIGIBLE An air ship that may be steered or guided.

DROUGHT A lack of rain.

EARTHQUAKE A shaking up of the Earth's surface due to volcanic activity or faults in the Earth's crust.

FAMINE A lack of food.

FAULT LINE Place in the Earth's crust where rock layers have broken loose and moved out of alignment.

GEYSER A hot spring near a volcano which spouts water.

HORSEPOWER A unit of measure reflecting the power that a horse exerts in pulling.

MAGMA Molten material from within the Earth which, when cooled, forms volcanic rock.

METEOR One of the small bodies in the solar system, which glows as it enters the Earth's atmosphere.

ORBIT The curved path that planets and other satellites follow.

PESTICIDE A substance (usually chemical) that destroys insects and other pests that attack plants.

PLAGUE A very contagious disease, usually fatal.

POLIO Short for Poliomyelitis, a disease of the nervous system which causes paralysis.

RADAR A system for finding out the direction and speed of moving objects.

RICHTER SCALE A scale that measures the strength of an earthquake.

SMALLPOX A sometimes fatal disease that leaves the skin scarred with red marks.

TELEGRAPH A message sent instantaneously by instruments connected by electricity.

TOXIN A poisonous substance.

TREMOR A vibrating or shaking movement or sound.

TSUNAMI An unusually large wave caused by an underwater earthquake.

TYPHOON A violent storm, occuring especially in the Pacific Ocean.

URANIUM A radioactive element used in nuclear weapons.

VOLCANO A hill or mountain, shaped like a cone, made of discharged matter, with openings through which pour steam, gases, and molten material.

INDEX

ABOUT THE CONTRIBUTORS

DAVID KELLER is the author of several works of fiction and works as an editor in New York City, where he lives with his wife and daughter.

RICK GEARY has worked as an illustrator and cartoonist for many years. His work frequently appears in the New York Times Book Review, and he has recently adapted Great Expectations into comics format for the Classics Illustrated series. He lives in New York City.

WILLIAM R. ALSCHULER, consultant, is the founder and principal of Future Museums, a museum consulting firm. He has a Ph.D. in astronomy from the University of California at Santa Cruz, and extensive university teaching experience in the sciences and energy conservation.

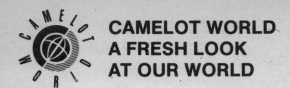

CAMELOT WORLD
A FRESH LOOK
AT OUR WORLD

THE MYSTERIOUS CAT
76038-X/$2.95 US/$3.50 Can

by Elizabeth Garrick

People have lived with cats for nearly four thousand years, yet they still remain a mystery. This book will tell you everything you want to know about cats, like why they purr and why they always fall on their feet.

HOT MACHINES
76039-8/$2.95 US/$3.50 Can

by Gregory Pope

Learn about the fastest, coolest, meanest vehicles on earth. From 1,400-miles-per-hour fighter jets to 200-miles-per-hour racecars, this book will take you on a tour of the most exciting land, sea, and air vehicles in the world.

SECRETS OF THE SAMURAI
76040-1/$2.95 US/$3.50 Can

by Carol Gaskin

For nearly 900 years, the best fighters in the world dominated the island of Japan. These were the samurai and the ninja, who terrorized their enemies with bow and arrow, spear and sword.

A KID'S GUIDE TO HOW TO SAVE THE PLANET
76041-X/$2.95 US/$3.50 Can

by Billy Goodman

In the last few decades, your home planet has been overwhelmed by a host of environmental problems like oil spills, acid rain, toxic waste, and the greenhouse effect. Read this book and find out how you can help.